SMART
LEADERSHIP

12 Simple Strategies
to Help You Shift from Ineffective Boss to
Brilliant
LEADER

BETH CALDWELL

PENNSYLVANIA FAMILY PUBLISHING

www.Smart-Leadership.net

SMART
LEADERSHIP

12 Simple
Strategies
to Help You Shift from Ineffective Boss to
Brilliant
LEADER

©2013 by Beth Caldwell and PA Family Publishing

Published by PA Family Publishing

Cover and Interior Design by **Daniel Szwedko Graphics**
Photo by **Archie Carpenter**

ISBN-13: 978-0615888507 (PA Family Publishing)
ISBN-10: 061588850X

To include any part of this book as a resource in your publication, for professional training, etc., contact **Beth Caldwell** at 412.202.6983 or info@smart-leadership.net.

Dedicated to:

My muse, motivator, confidant and best friend.
Thank you for believing in me.

Diane

Always Be Brilliant!

Beta Caldwell

Introduction

Today's leadership is about guiding a team, not being a boss. When you work as a boss, you choose to be responsible for all tasks, either because you don't trust your staff to do as good a job as you, or because you want credit. The problem is that you're working alone, and when you're out of time and energy, you're exhausted and have a dysfunctional team that can't operate without you. When you have a team of people working together to achieve a common goal, your power, influence and profitability are multiplied many times over.

In the early part of the 20th century company leaders were trained to be authoritative commanders. Employees were expected to come to work, do their job and go home. Productivity and profits were the concern of management, not workers. Today's fast paced world demands better, faster service and our younger generation is not at all motivated by authoritative and demanding supervisors. If you want to produce an exceptional product and be better, faster, and smarter than your competition, you need a team of excellent people to help you get there - **and stay there.**

This informative book is designed to help you move out of the role of "boss" and into the role of "leader" so that you can increase your profits, work fewer hours, and enjoy the time you spend at work.

Contents

Chapter One
DEVELOP A STRONG TEAM

The best executive is the one who has sense enough to pick good men to do what he wants done, and self-restraint enough to keep from meddling with them while they do it.   - Theodore Roosevelt

Smart leaders understand and develop their key strengths. For years, men and women have modeled behaviors after their supervisors to try to fit the mold of company leader. Stop doing that! Then, stop expecting your team to do the same.

We each have unique strengths, traits and characteristics that are core to our individual behavioral and leadership style. You spend a lot of hours at work. In fact, it's likely that you spend more hours at work than any other life activity. Most of the people that I work with already have a very clear understanding of their core strengths and are keenly aware of their weak areas. Hopefully you are already doing work that aligns with your innate values and are enjoying a career where you're able to use your natural talents. To shift your team from one that is dysfunctional and unproductive, you need to make

sure that each team member is also working in a
position that utilizes his or her strength.

Think about your team right now. Does it consist of a
balance of personalities who can share the workload
easily and effectively? Ideally you should have one
leader for every vital function of your business. That
leader should be an expert at their function and be
wildly talented and enthusiastic about the part they play.
Your role, as the leader, is to oversee the experts.

Who loves to come to work, enjoys what they do, is
productive, effective and positive? Now think about the
staff that is unproductive, inefficient, difficult and
problematic. Does their negative behavior effect other
members of the team? What is the cause of their
distress?

I have a colleague, Kathryn, who travels around the
country helping companies to hire the right talent. She
tells me, "Asking someone to do a job day in and day
out that is opposite of their inherent strengths is like
asking them to walk on their hands. They can do it for a
while, but eventually they are going to crash."

Consider the work style and the current success rate of
your team. You don't need to hire an expensive
consulting team and commission a study. Just give it
some thought. Do you have the right people in the right
positions? Do changes need to be made? Do you have
a lopsided team? Have you hired a group of people
that all have the same strengths and find challenges with
the same issues? Many leaders like to hire people who
are just like them. Most of us enjoy hanging around
people that are like us. It's comfortable. We understand
one another.

I was having lunch recently with a colleague who works at a bank. She had not been to her office for several days due to a number of branch issues. I complimented her that her staff was able to work efficiently with no direct supervision. She told me that she'd learned the hard way a long time ago that it's important to hire people who can work independently and as a part of a team. She said, "Please don't be offended, but early in my career I made the mistake of hiring a branch full of women just like you. It was the biggest mess I ever created." I laughed because I understood. When I first launched my company I also hired people who were just like me, and while we made great friends and enjoyed being creative and having fun, a lot of work was left incomplete. Employees leave at the end of the day whether the work is completed or not, so I often had to skip family events and work late hours to make up for lost time "working" with my friends.

If you have an ineffective team, ask yourself, "Do I have the right people doing the right work?" If you've hired the wrong person, don't expect them to change and be happy. Ask your team for input and together you can brainstorm solutions to take you from where you are to where you want to be. From now on, hire people who fit the job opening and who are likely to stay with you a long time because they enjoy their work.

Remember:

INSTEAD OF EXPECTING PEOPLE TO ADAPT TO A POSITION, LEARN HOW TO INCORPORATE THE STRENGTHS OF THE PERSON TO THE RESULTS YOU'RE LOOKING FOR.

Think About It

Think about your team right now. Does it consist of a balance of personalities who can share the workload easily and effectively? Ideally you should have one expert for every vital function of your business.

What are the main functions of your business and who's in charge there? Do you have the right people in the right positions?

Person	Position
_____	_____
_____	_____
_____	_____
_____	_____
_____	_____
_____	_____
_____	_____
_____	_____

Consider the strengths of everyone on your team. Do you have a lot of people with the same strengths? What positions need to be reinforced?

Person	Strength/Talent
_____	_____
_____	_____
_____	_____
_____	_____
_____	_____
_____	_____
_____	_____
_____	_____

Smart leaders surround themselves with top talent. Leading a team of dynamic and innovative people will only improve your business.

Chapter Two
NEVER STOP LEARNING

Leadership and learning are indispensable to each other.

— John F. Kennedy

Smart leaders never stop learning. The best leaders are lifelong learners who continually educate themselves and their teams to be cutting edge.

Most of the clients that I work with understand and appreciate the importance of learning. If you're constantly learning then you're constantly improving. Learning is a key difference between a boss and a leader. The leader understands that learning needs to be incorporated into your schedule. Reading trade journals, listening to recorded workshops and attending seminars are a part of their regular routine.

Bosses don't attend workshops or conferences and will usually give these excuses:

"I can't leave the office during the day."

"They can't be left alone, I need to be here in case something goes wrong."

"I'm just too busy, I'm very behind and I have a lot to catch up on."

Leaders trust their teams to handle things while they are away. If you don't do this, you are robbing your team of the opportunity to lead. You're also missing out on learning and improving yourself and your business. It's tough to relinquish control if you're used to being the go-to problem solver and chief decision maker.

If you haven't been learning, then make a plan to integrate this important tool back into your regular routine. Begin by blocking time in your calendar to read industry journals, business journals and the email newsletters that have helpful information in them. A little reading every day is easier than reading it all at once, but do what works best for you.

Take a look at the meetings, conferences and workshops being offered by the organizations that you belong to and the ones that offer the best education for your industry. Decide which events are important for you to attend and put them on your calendar. While you're looking at these events, select some for your team to attend also, on their own or with you. This is an excellent opportunity to get them into the habit of lifelong learning.

Take advantage of podcasts, webinars and tele-classes that can be listened to while you're at your desk, too. Technology allows you to be more informed than ever before.

Smart leaders are always learning, so make sure that you're well informed, well educated and up-to-date on the daily tasks of your company. Fully understanding the jobs and tasks of your staff will not only help you to succeed in business, but also excel as a leader.

Remember:
WHILE YOU'RE DECIDING WHICH CONFERENCES AND WORKSHOPS TO ATTEND, CHOOSE SOME TO SEND YOUR TEAM TO ALSO. THIS IS AN EXCELLENT OPPORTUNITY TO GET THEM INTO THE HABIT OF LIFELONG LEARNING.

Chapter Three
STOP DOING

*The real leader has no need to lead - he is content to
point the way.* - Henry Miller

**Smart leaders resist doing the work of everyone on the
team.** Bosses usually require that all decisions are made
by them and often do work that really should be done
by employees. If you want to become a leader, you'll
need to carefully remove yourself from tasks that can be
(and should be) done by others. Just because you know
how to do everything doesn't mean you have to.

Begin paying attention to each task that you complete
during the day. Ask yourself, "Do I really need to be the
one doing this?" Create a list of all the tasks that you do
that could be done by someone else. This is an
important first step in delegating responsibilities.
Although it may seem tedious to actually write out a list,
this is a valuable tool to help you understand how you
spend your time. You will be surprised by the amount
of time you spend doing things that could be handled
just as easily by others. Don't beat yourself up during this
process. Instead, focus on this positive aspect: you are

going to be building the self esteem of your team when you begin delegating important responsibilities to them.

If you're having trouble coming up with your list of items to delegate, try this. Make a list of the tasks that only you can do. Compare those to the hours you have available to work. Delegate everything else.

When you begin to delegate important tasks, you'll notice an immediate change in your work environment. Here are some of the positive things that can occur when you delegate:

- Employees will develop a sense of pride because you trust them.
- You'll notice increased teamwork within your organization.
- Employees will have a greater understanding of the overall business.
- You'll have more time to focus on other important matters.
- You'll be able to spend more time doing the things that only you can do.
- You'll work less hours.

I hope that delegating is something that you can implement easily. Almost everyone I work with has a really tough time with this concept. Let me share some tips that will make the process easier.

If you've never delegated, your staff may resist taking on additional responsibilities. They may resent an additional workload or they may fear that they're not qualified to handle the task. Here is a good way to introduce the new responsibility: *"Tom, as you know our department is responsible for seeing that the XYZ report is completed each month. I'd like to give that responsibility to you on a trial basis for the next few months. You are the company expert on the topic and I think it makes sense that you take over this project. Can we give this a try for the next few months? I've arranged for John in accounting to go over the procedure with you. I think you'll find this very easy to integrate alongside the work you're currently doing. If you have any trouble with the report, check with John first. Then if you still need help, ask me for assistance."*

Ideally, John will enthusiastically take over the task and do a great job for you. After 3 months you can review the results, congratulate him and add additional responsibilities. If John doesn't do a great job, resist the urge to take the task back. Instead, ask John, "How can we make this process better, John?". Hopefully John knows something you don't and will be able to come up with a solution. If, after 4 months, things aren't excellent, you may have to delegate the task to someone else, but don't give up.

Remember:
DON'T GIVE UP ON DELEGATING
IF IT DOESN'T WORK RIGHT AWAY. YOU MAY
NEED TO TRY DELEGATING DIFFERENT TASKS
WITH DIFFERENT PEOPLE UNTIL YOU FIND THE
RIGHT PERSON FOR THE RIGHT JOB.

Until now, you may have created a dysfunctional team by teaching your staff to come to you for approval on every decision. It will take some time to re-train yourself and your team. Resist the urge to be involved in every conversation and every decision. Determine which decisions they can make without you and which situations require your input and approval. Gather your team together as a group or individually and say something like this, "Susan, from now on, when a customer has an issue that you can handle without me, I want you to go ahead and solve the problem on your own. You've been with us long enough to understand our values and our customer service standards. I don't think you need my approval anymore. Unless your decision will cost the company more than $500, you don't need to check with me."

Susan may feel timid in the beginning, so she may come to you the first few times for approval. When she does, instead of telling her what to do, ask her, "What do you think will be the best solution?" After this happens a few times, she'll gain the confidence she needs to handle future situations on her own.

Acknowledge the strengths of each individual team member when you increase their responsibilities. Delegation is a very important step in moving from a boss to a leader. When you're a boss, you're doing what's best for you. When you're a leader, you're doing what's best for the company. By increasing expectations you are building confidence, helping your people achieve goals and multiplying your productivity.

If something isn't working in your office, and you don't know why, ask your team. A boss will try and figure things out alone, an executive may call a meeting of other executives, but a wise leader will ask the people doing the work. They are your best resource and can usually point out the best solutions.

Smart leaders understand that a title does not make a leader. Recognize that a confident and competent team will lead to increased results, better teamwork and more success for your company.

Chapter Four

CREATE A POSITIVE WORK ENVIRONMENT

Be a yardstick of quality. Some people aren't used to an environment where excellence is expected. - Steve Jobs

Smart leaders create and thrive in a positive work environment. A positive work environment has a significant impact on employee morale and performance, as does a negative work environment. Do everything that you can to maximize the performance and potential of your team.

A positive work environment allows teams to thrive, so take control of your workplace culture. How can you eliminate negativity and create a positive and productive workplace?

Sometimes we're so busy working we don't notice the piles of clutter that have accumulated.

A negative workplace creates low morale, and that's expensive. It could be costing you sales, clients, staff and productivity.

Here are some changes you can implement immediately. The good news is that these ideas won't cost you a lot of money or make anyone uncomfortable.

Update lighting. A dark workspace can deplete creativity and cause low energy. Extra bright lights can make people feel edgy and nervous. Take advantage of natural light or install lighting to brighten up key areas of your workspace for a happier and more positive feel. Newer, more efficient lighting can actually save you money in energy costs.

Modernize your decor. I recently visited a busy medical company that needed help with an over-stressed staff that was undermining one another. While waiting, I noticed the photos on the walls were from the 1976

Olympic games! Among other problems, the energy in the office reflected the decor: outdated, shabby and worn. Make sure your workspace walls reflect the overall feeling you want to project with staff and customers. I recommend inspirational photos or motivational quotes.

Clean up the clutter. Some of us have it on our desks. Others have it creatively hidden in a drawer or closet. Consider a group clean up. Block a half day on the calendar and cater lunch in. Encourage everyone to sort through their stacks, shred and recycle. Locate a school or nonprofit that would appreciate books and office supplies no longer needed. Everyone will feel better and be more productive in a clear space.

Create collaborative areas. Many people, especially generation X and Y, do not function at their best when in a cubicle, small office or corporate conference room. Take some of the furniture crammed into your current office space and relocate it into a hallway, store room or break room. Add some lamps, trendy art, and you have a new collaborative workspace.

Play soft music. Workplace music has been used for centuries to increase productivity and improve alertness. I recommend that you turn off the television in the lunchroom or reception area and opt for something that will instead inspire creativity and calm.

Remember:
SCHEDULE A COMPANY CLEAN UP DAY. BLOCK A HALF DAY FOR A GROUP CLEAN UP. CATER LUNCH IN. WITH TEAMWORK, YOU'LL SOON ENJOY A CLUTTER-FREE AND MORE PRODUCTIVE WORKSPACE.

Smart leaders take control of their culture by eliminating the things that cause a negative atmosphere and ensuring that the workplace is pleasant and productive for everyone.

Chapter Five

COMMUNICATE WITH PURPOSE

"The difference between the right word and the almost right word is the difference between lightning and a lightning bug."
                                                      - Mark Twain

Smart leaders communicate with purpose. As a leader, it's important to establish your credibility and influence by being an excellent communicator. Certainly people need to understand what's expected of them and their role within your team, but purposeful communication is far more than how you speak. Consider all the ways that you communicate besides speaking. What messages do you communicate to your team through your:

Appearance _____

Expressions_____

Tone of voice_____

Speed of delivery_____

Mood_____

21

Now, consider all the ways that you communicate with your staff:

Speaking one on one   Speaking in a meeting
Speaking in small groups   Email
Voice Messages   Text Messages
Inter-office systems   Written Memos
Reports   Presentations

_____   _____

_____   _____

_____   _____

It's vitally important as a leader that you communicate with confidence in every manner. Remember in chapter two we talked about attending conferences and workshops? If you need to build confidence in your presentation skills, speaking, etc. then I encourage you to look for workshops and courses that will help. Check the resources chapter at the end of this book for some suggestions.

It's important that you communicate confidently.

Purposeful Meetings

When you're hosting a meeting, do you communicate the purpose of the meeting and offer a clear agenda? Do you stick to the schedule, or do other people insert their own agendas? Think now of some areas where communication can be improved.

_____

_____

_____

_____

_____

_____

Purposeful Emails

When you send an email, make sure that your message is clear and concise. Don't include excess information which will waste time, and don't be vague, which will require a response from them and another response from you (more wasted time). Before sending an email message, re-read it and imagine that you're the recipient. Sometimes when we're writing, we know exactly what we mean, but brief messages can cause confusion.

Here is an example from one of my client's email files. This example illustrates how poor email communication caused a very frustrating situation between a sales rep and a graphic designer. Ultimately, the business owner had to pay overtime, delay a sales meeting and sit in on the delayed meeting to avoid losing the client.

Hi Tina, thanks for sending me the sample ad campaign. My favorite is number three, and I like photo number seven, but I think we'll need to rework the color scheme. When is the meeting with the client?

Jen

Hi Jen, sorry, I have been away from the office and I'm behind on emails. Which client are you referring to?

Tina

Hi Tina,

The Featherstone Account. When is the meeting?

Jen

Jen, Featherstone? That is not one of my assignments. I'm not sure what you're referring to.

Tina

Tina, please call me. I just checked the calendar and we have a meeting tomorrow at 9:45am with the Heatherstone Account. Sorry for the typo on earlier email. I hope you don't have anything planned, because we'll both be working late tonight.

Jen

Obviously, both women could have done a better job with communication. When people are busy they tend to rush and dash off emails in a hurry. Rushing usually results in even more wasted time. Be a role model to your team by sending emails that are well crafted, complete and easy to understand.

Remember:
TAKE ADVANTAGE OF THE "SIGNATURE" OPTION IN YOUR EMAIL ACCOUNT. ADD YOUR FULL NAME AND COMPLETE CONTACT INFORMATION SO THAT IT WILL BE AUTOMATICALLY ADDED TO EACH EMAIL THAT YOU SEND.

Purposeful Team Communication

Be sure that everyone on your team understands their role in the company's success. It's up to you to communicate their importance and that you value their individual contributions. Each team member should also clearly understand what the company does and why. It may have been many years since some of your employees started to work for you. Have things changed since they were hired? Sometimes when changes are made, upper management fails to communicate new policies and company direction to everyone. This is a mistake. When people don't feel vital or necessary to the company, they'll begin to practice "presenteeism". They're physically present, but their mind is absent.

MISSION STATEMENT

"Our purpose as a company is to be a resource to our industry. We will accomplish this through knowledgeable, highly skilled people, who are committed to integrity, and to identifying and responding to our customers' needs with appropriate solutions."

I encourage you to communicate your company purpose, company values and team goals with your employees often, and especially during times of change. When everyone is involved in a common goal, you'll create an atmosphere of devotion and loyalty.

Smart leaders establish credibility and influence with excellent communication.

Chapter Six
MAKE UP YOUR MIND

*Stop asking for advice when you already know exactly
what you need to do.* - Doreen Rainey

**Smart leaders make quick, competent decisions and act
on them.** Being a decision maker is an important part
of leadership, but it's not always a natural trait. People
avoid making decisions because they want to avoid
making mistakes. Whether your decision is large or small,
failure to act is failure to move.

If you are a person who avoids risk, you may tend to be
an information gatherer. You may feel the need to
gather information and evaluate your options. Sometimes
the "I need more information" response is actually a way
to prolong or avoid the decision making process.

Think of it this way; when you don't make a choice
you're actually making the decision:

- Not to participate
- Not to grow
- Not to risk
- Not to move forward

27

Are those options any better than the possibility of making a mistake?

Prolonging decision making waste times and will frustrate the people you lead. This may also cause unnecessary worry among your staff. If you are not confident in your decision making, they will be hesitant to support you. When you make clear and confident decisions, your team will feel clear and confident.

When I'm struggling with a decision, I'll often decide to just get started. I remind myself that I can always change direction once we get moving. It's important to trust yourself to make the right decisions, and eventually you'll be able to trust your team members to do the same.

Here are some tips to help you become a confident decision maker:

1. Set a deadline for the decision to be made.
2. Remind yourself of your company mission statement and values. Is the decision in alignment? If not, then your choice is an easy one.
3. Ask smart questions, the kind that will reveal potential problems. For example, if you're making a decision to purchase new equipment, instead of asking the

salesperson, "How is this working for other companies?" ask, "What problems have other buyers had with this type of equipment?"

4. Delegate the information gathering. Have a meeting to discuss all of the information, then ask your team for their input.
5. Rely on logic, not emotion. Don't allow fear of what others think or what may go wrong keep you from moving forward.
6. Trust yourself to make the right choice and to make changes if necessary.

Smart leaders don't put off making decisions. If you're the type of person who avoids decision making, it will take some courage to change, but it will become easier with practice. Decisiveness is an important leadership skill and it's a trait that many people admire.

Remember:

DON'T PUT OFF MAKING DECISIONS. MAKE DECISIONS AND IMPLEMENT THEM. YOUR COMPANY WILL NOT MOVE FORWARD IF YOU FAIL TO BE DECISIVE OR NEGLECT FOLLOW-THROUGH. REMEMBER, YOU CAN ALWAYS CHANGE DIRECTION ONCE YOU GET STARTED.

Chapter Seven

MANAGE YOUR LIFE INSTEAD OF YOUR TIME

It is absurd that a man should rule others, who cannot rule himself.
                                                  - Latin Proverb

Smart leaders manage life, not time. How many time management classes have you attended? Sometimes I meet with clients who tell me, "If I could just manage my time better, I'd get so much more done." I nod and smile as I look at their calendar filled with endless projects, tasks and meetings.

This is a great lesson that I love to teach. I sit across the table from a client and say, "OK, this is your calendar for the week. Let's get out a clean piece of paper and see if we can manage your time in a way that will help you get all of this accomplished." I have them read the tasks to me and I write them all down. Then I read them back and say, "Let me ask you a question. If I hired you as a consultant, and I showed you this list and told you that I had to have all of these projects completed in one week, what would you say to me?" Almost always the response is, "That's ridiculous."

The first step to re-gaining control of your time is becoming aware of what's really possible to accomplish in the time you have.

Recognize the difference between what you want to do and what is practical to achieve given your time availability. Be sure to allow enough time to complete the tasks that need to be done by you and empower your team by delegating the rest. Your example (good or bad) of how to manage yourself will have a ripple effect on your team, so be a great time/ life management role model.

Create your to do list and prioritize. I like to create my to-do list at the end of the day instead of in the morning. This allows me to keep focused on my goals and avoid day-to-day dilemmas. I can come into my office and quickly assess what needs to be done. Whenever possible, I attack that to-do list before reading email or listening to phone messages. It feels great to get important tasks finished early in the day.

Guard your time and stop being accessible to everyone. When you're working, close your door. Open-door policies, while warm, fuzzy and friendly, are a time waster. If your door is open to everyone then everyone will come through it. I usually block off two hour chunks in my calendar throughout the week in order to complete my work. After two hours, I need a short break. There is not a lot that can happen that will require your immediate assistance during that time period. If people have to wait an hour to ask you a question, they'll often find the solution on their own.

Remember:
YOUR EXAMPLE (GOOD OR BAD) OF HOW TO MANAGE YOURSELF WILL HAVE A RIPPLE EFFECT ON YOUR TEAM, SO BE A GREAT TIME/ LIFE MANAGEMENT ROLE MODEL.

Stop answering the phone. If possible, mute the ringer. People who cannot come to visit you will often call with questions. Check your messages several times during the day and return important phone calls promptly.

Stop solving problems that can be solved without you. If your staff has a problem that needs solving, avoid the temptation to solve the problem for them. Instead, ask, "What solutions have you tried?" They may not have a response for you. You can reply with, "Let's try this. I have a deadline that I need to focus on right now. Try to come up with two possible options and we can discuss this again tomorrow. I can talk to you for ten minutes at 8:45 am." It won't take them long to begin to solve problems without you.

Shift to shorter meetings. Stop scheduling 30 minute and 60 minute meetings. Instead schedule 10 minute or 20 minute briefings, and if possible do them on the phone or by web meeting. Begin each meeting by announcing the end time of the meeting and the purpose of the meeting. This will remind attendees to stay on topic.

Delegate items that don't need your full attention. In order for your business to prosper, you'll need to spend a good portion of your time strategically growing the business and increasing sales, not solving day-to-day dilemmas.

It's really important that you understand all processes of your business, but not necessary that you are the one who completes all tasks. A true leader is one who empowers others. Understand your key processes, but don't micromanage. Let your team know that you trust them to complete tasks as well as you do.

What items/tasks /projects can you delegate? Use this area to brainstorm:

_____   _____

_____   _____

_____   _____

_____   _____

_____   _____

_____   _____

_____   _____

_____   _____

_____   _____

Stop being immersed in email

Email, used wisely, can be a tremendous time saving tool. With email, you can communicate efficiently and spend less time in meetings and on the phone. I've always appreciated being able to reply to emails during off hours which leaves me more time during the day when I can focus on income producing activities. Clogged inboxes can become stressful and overwhelming and can quickly zap your time. Keep your email working efficiently so that you don't experience inbox overwhelm.

1. Empty your inbox. You can do this by deleting a certain number of emails each day or you can just create a folder called "old emails" and move all emails there, so you can find something there if you need to.
2. Unsubscribe all non-work related subscriptions from your account. Let them go to a personal account and access them during non-working hours.
3. Setup an email schedule that works for you. There is no one-size fits all schedule, so determine how often you need to reply/respond to email messages in order to allow you to be most effective. For a while I tried to do emails in the morning or evening only, and that did not work for me. Now I try to check in three times a day.
4. If you do send emails during off hours, use the "schedule for later" function and setup the email to be sent the next business day during work hours. Just because you work evenings and weekends doesn't mean that other people have to as well.
5. If possible, do not check email until you've tackled your important to do list for the day.

Remember:

IF YOU NEED TO CHECK EMAIL IN THE MORNING, USE THE "SORT" FEATURE. SORT ALL NEW EMAILS BY SENDER, AND SCAN THE LIST FOR THE NAMES OF THE PEOPLE YOU NEED TO COMMUNICATE WITH NOW. YOU CAN ALSO "FLAG" YOUR VIP CLIENTS IN YOUR EMAIL SYSTEM SO THAT THEY STAND OUT WHEN YOU'RE SKIMMING YOUR INBOX.

Smart leaders know that if you are scattered, over-booked and overwhelmed, you won't be effective and you won't gain the respect of your team.

Chapter Eight
DON'T HIDE FROM CONFLICT

Leaders do not avoid, repress, or deny conflict, but rather see it as an opportunity. — Warren Bennis

Smart leaders deal with difficult situations. It takes courage to face conflict. I've learned over and over again that avoiding conflict ultimately lands you in an even worse situation.

I was once told that difficult situations are simply an opportunity for growth. I remember one very difficult summer in the early years of my business when I felt so frustrated. I remember saying out loud, "Do I really need any more personal growth this year?"

I've worked with clients (and for some) where the leadership skirted conflict. They avoided uncomfortable situations and ignored serious problems. I've never seen a problem improve by evasiveness. In fact, what usually happens when leaders ignore conflict is this:

- Loss of productivity
- Loss of creativity
- Loss of business

- Loss of quality staff
- Loss of money
- Increased conflict
- Increased frustration
- Increased resentment

Almost any workplace and relationship is going to experience conflict. Understand and accept that, as a leader, conflict is a part of your role. I want you to be an excellent role model. Ask yourself, "What message do I want to send about how I deal with conflict?"

When dealing with conflict how would I like to be perceived?

Sincere	Passive
Resolute	Complacent
With integrity	Insensitive
Straightforward	Untrustworthy
Unshaken	Fearful
Willing to Compromise	Irrational
Compassionate	Self-Centered
Ready to Listen	Quarrelsome
Forgiving	Stern
Flexible	Disagreeable
Firm	Meek
Strong	Submissive
Sensible	Unrealistic
Confident	Wavering

Before you deal with a difficult or stressful situation, take time to center yourself. Determine an acceptable outcome. For example, an employee has a negative attitude and an intolerable ego. A boss will call a meeting with the employee, point out the undesirable activity and demand that the behavior stop. A leader will assess the entire situation and attempt to determine the cause of the problem. Instead of causing additional strife by demanding new behavior, set a standard for the type of conduct you want to see. This is far more productive and measurable. Consider this potential conversation:

Leader: "Jane, thank you for coming in. I want to discuss the conflict that's been happening between you and John. It's been upsetting to you, I know, and the effect is spilling over to the rest of the office. You and John are both valued members of our team, and it's currently my plan that you both remain as a part of the organization. I've already spoken to John and he agrees that the conflict is unproductive and frustrating for both of you. He's agreed to be more patient and to refrain from complaining. I'd like to talk with you to see what you can do to resolve your part in the disagreement so that we can get back to working as a team and reinstate the company business as our main priority from now on."

When dealing with emotions, it's impossible to script a perfect conversation. Therefore, it's important that you center yourself before the meeting and determine the intended outcome. Write it down, so you can refer to it if and when the conversation gets redirected to a "he said/she said" or "it wasn't my fault" routine. Decide how much time you'll allow for the entire conversation. Set an end time at the beginning and stick to the topic at hand. As the leader, you need to remain in control and continue to steer the conversation back to your intended purpose.

If this is a new habit that you're creating, it may take some time for the team to become adjusted to your new standards, but remain consistent.

I strongly recommend that you deal with conflict as soon as it arises, and especially when dealing with difficult employees. Negative and harmful attitudes can be contagious and usually don't become better as years go on. Do not allow them to damage your productivity and profits.

Remember:
ADDRESS DIFFICULT SITUATIONS IMMEDIATELY. DO NOT ALLOW THEM TO DAMAGE YOUR PRODUCTIVITY AND PROFITS.

The more experience you have addressing conflict, the more confidence you'll gain. Eventually you'll be able to recognize the early warning signs of conflict and take measures to prevent major problems before they happen, saving everyone a lot of stress, especially you.

Smart leaders react quickly to conflict. When conflict occurs resist the urge to avoid it, and remind yourself that it won't go away. You'll feel better and the entire office will appreciate your swift action.

Chapter Nine
BECOME COMFORTABLE WITH CRITICISM

Criticism is an indirect form of self-boasting.   - Emmet Fox

Smart leaders are frequently criticized and often make others uncomfortable. This is something that I have struggled with since the beginning of my career. We all want to be appreciated and accepted and criticism is tough to hear. I've learned that most criticism is unfounded, although some of it can be helpful. I've learned how to sift through criticism to discern if it's worth my time or emotion.

There are two types of criticism, relevant and irrelevant. Relevant criticism usually comes from someone who loves you, cares about you or wants the best for you. Irrelevant criticism comes from people who feel uncomfortable or threatened by your actions or ideas. Remember that irrelevant criticism is usually meant to hurt you and is not something that you should allow to occupy your time or attention.

When you receive criticism the first thing to remember

is that what you're hearing is another person's opinion. Their opinion may have no relevance whatsoever on you or your project. Like all other types of conflict, when you hear criticism about you, your company, or your project, the first thing you want to do is remove emotion and be objective. In order to do this, you may have to respond to the critic at a later time to give you some time to think it over and respond appropriately, if at all. Recognize that the negative comment does not define who you are - it defines who they are.

Keep in mind that the person in front is the one who gets the most attention. When you set yourself apart from others, they are likely to talk about you. I've discovered that, as leaders, we often make people feel uncomfortable, whether it's about themselves or their position in the company. Often leaders initiate change and change makes people very nervous. When people feel nervous, threatened or insecure, they will become defensive and often unleash a string of criticism.

Recognize that negative comments do not define who you are - they define your critic.

Strategies for dealing with criticism:

Understand your purpose. When you are clear about your purpose, it's easier to be discerning about criticism. This has been the best tool for me personally. I used to listen to and try to implement every suggestion that I received and eventually I discovered that many people make suggestions based on their agendas, not mine. When I receive "helpful advice" about one of my books, projects or programs, before considering it, I remind myself what my purpose is. If their comments do not align, I don't consider their suggestion. Instead, I reply with something like this, *"Thanks so much for your suggestion. This project is specifically designed to_____, so we're going to keep things as is. I value your input and appreciate your continued support."*

Ask yourself, "Is this information helpful or hurtful?" There will be times in your career when you'll receive information that may seem hurtful or critical. Is the person speaking intending to hurt you or help you? Though it may not seem like it, comments are often said with good intentions and are meant to help you. When this happens, consider their information and ask yourself if it makes sense to listen to what they are saying.

Determine if the criticism is about you personally or about your company, idea or project. Often we become emotionally attached to our ideas and projects. Is the person criticizing you or the company / project? If you truly want the project / company to be exceptional, then consider the criticism and remember that it's not about you, even if it feels that way.

Acknowledge your strengths and your flaws. I remember the first time that I admitted publicly that I'm terrible with spreadsheets. Charts, graphs, statistics, accounting and numbers in general just don't excite me. When it came time for me to complete tasks using a spreadsheet, I dreaded it and would procrastinate on the project until I absolutely had to do it, usually requiring me to work late. Eventually, I had the courage to admit my flaw and delegate the project. I practiced my speech and at the next team meeting I nervously announced. "Folks, I've been doing a lot of thinking and the monthly accounting reports are a real challenge for me. I've decided that this is a task I'm going to delegate to Kyle, who is really gifted in accounting and who can complete the task far better than I can." The response was laughter and applause. "It's about time", everyone teased. Even if you are not aware of your weaknesses, the people close to you are, so you don't need to be embarrassed to admit your flaws. When you receive criticism, ask yourself if you are trying to excel in your areas of weakness. If so, someone may have just pointed out to you a new item to delegate.

Remember:

WHEN YOU UNDERSTAND YOUR PURPOSE, IT'S MUCH EASIER TO DEAL WITH CRITICISM. COMPARE THE CRITICISM TO YOUR PURPOSE. IF THE CRITICISM DOES NOT ALIGN WITH YOUR INTENTIONS, LET IT GO.

Determine if the problem is about you or them. Sometimes people are hyper-sensitive to their own weaknesses, so they notice them in everyone else. I've received a lot of this type of criticism via email. People dash off a "thought" or a "helpful tip" for me that makes absolutely no sense at all. Communication by email and voice mail gives people the opportunity to rant and vent without any repercussion. If what they are saying is simply wrong and unfounded, ignore it.

Appreciate the fears of others. Leaders often introduce change and change makes people very uncomfortable. People resist being taken from their comfort zones, and as the leader, it's your job to reassure them. "I understand, Susan, that you feel nervous about _____, but the important thing to remember is that _____ is in the best interest of the company. I feel confident that this is a positive change for the entire company."

Smart leaders understand that innovation and change make many people uncomfortable. Often, your team will not want to accept changes or be taken from their comfort zones. As a good leader it's your job to listen and understand their concerns, but ultimately make the best decision for the company.

Chapter Ten

LEARN TO NEGOTIATE

Got a problem? Try to negotiate.   - Margaret Neale

Smart leaders do not fear negotiation. When I discuss this topic with colleagues, everyone seems to fear negotiation. Recently, I observed a group of women discussing the negative aspects of negotiation. I realized that they were focusing all of their energy on the FEAR of negotiating. They did not want to appear aggressive, nor did they want to argue or experience conflict.

As leaders, we negotiate in some way almost every day, often on behalf of others. Notice how quickly you respond when there is a need to negotiate an invoice or contract on behalf of your company or when your favorite charity needs pricing discounts. Catch yourself negotiating when it benefits others and notice your strengths. Pay attention, also, to the times when you avoid negotiating.

Your fear and avoidance of negotiation may be harming you. What benefits or promotions have you missed out on because you did not ask? What benefits may you gain for yourself or your company if you strengthen your negotiating skills? Consider this; negotiation is just another word for creative problem solving. Do the words creative problem solving scare you? Of course not. We just associate the word negotiation with intimidating situations. Stop doing that. As a leader, it's your job to creatively solve problems and find solutions that work for all involved.

I think that the reason most of us fear negotiating is because we think we're about to enter a win or lose situation. MJ Tocci, co-founder of the Negotiation Academy for Women, taught me to look at negotiating as a win/win situation. "Stop thinking that when you're negotiating, someone has to win and someone has to lose", she says. "Instead, ask yourself how you can both come away from the negotiation as winners."

Before you begin a negotiation, ask yourself these questions:

1. What outcome will be most advantageous for me?
2. What outcome will I be able to accept?
3. What common ground do I share with my counterpart?
4. What requests do they have that I can accommodate?

5. Is there an outcome that will satisfy both of us?
6. What solutions can I offer to create a win for all?

Being prepared and well-informed will give you confidence. Recognize that during negotiation people will often ask for more than they really want and will also ask you for more concessions than they really expect. Remain confident and unruffled. A pleasantly persistent attitude is not offensive and shows that you mean business. Try to leave emotion out of your discussion and stay focused on your objective.

Remember:
NEGOTIATION IS JUST ANOTHER WORD FOR CREATIVE PROBLEM SOLVING.

Smart leaders do not avoid negotiation. Practice negotiating as often as you can, so that you'll gain confidence. Remember that negotiation is simply communication that endeavors to solve a problem in a win-win manner for all parties involved. Smart leaders are smart problem solvers.

Chapter Eleven

SIMPLE APPRECIATION

We often feed the critic gourmet meals and starve the rest....   - Angeles Arrien

Smart leaders understand that appreciating their team creates loyalty, teamwork and a sense of pride in the company. Showing appreciation at work may seem sentimental or emotional to you but there is a place for appreciation at work. In fact, when you want to be a competitive employer, appreciation may be the most powerful tool in your leadership arsenal.

I'm not suggesting that you begin excessively complimenting everyone at work and acknowledging every action they take. Appreciating your staff is not something that you can add to your to-do list. It's not a task to do; it's a way to be.

We often get so busy doing our jobs that we forget to acknowledge the wins that are being gained by ourselves and our staff. Try to remember to acknowledge them and yourself whenever you can. Here are some tips:

Acknowledge innovation, cooperation, positive attitudes, values and creativity. When you're thanking someone, specifically acknowledge how you admire that trait. Example: "Susan and John, I want you to know that I really appreciate you solving that weekend crisis for our client. The fact that you worked overtime and had to work with an outside vendor not only secured future business, but it also upholds the values of our company by ensuring that the clients never have to deal with a crisis alone. Nice work."

Instill confidence. Many leaders don't realize how important it is to instill confidence in their team members. Lack of confidence is deadly to your bottom line. Your people need to have confidence in themselves and their company in order to make important decisions. Allow people to work independently as well as a part of a team. As they garner more experience and enjoy successes, their confidence will increase.

Celebrate success. Many leaders skimp on celebration because they feel like it's bragging. Don't make this mistake. This is one part of an appreciation plan that you can put on your to-do list. Pick one day a month to celebrate successes. Treat for lunch, let them go home early, give them a nice gift (not a pen or mug with your logo), take them bowling, to a sporting event, paintball, whatever motivates them. The activity should be enjoyable for the majority. Do it on company time, mix it up and let them know that this is your appreciation for their contributions. Trust me, genuine appreciation will pay for itself in company loyalty over and over again.

Here is a list of creative ways to appreciate your employees:

- Parking Privileges
- Support of their favorite charity
- Credit Union Membership
- Tuition reimbursement
- Direct Deposit
- Attain company discounts for them for products such as cell phones, electronics, automobiles or other luxury items.
- Give free business cards
- Professional Title
- Wellness Plan
- Non-credit educational courses available at work during lunch or after work
- Employee Assistance Programs (EAP)
- Treat for breakfast or lunch
- Time off

What are some additional ways that you can show appreciation to your team?

_____   _____

_____   _____

_____   _____

_____   _____

_____   _____

_____   _____

_____   _____

Delegate these tasks to the appropriate person right away, or put these items in your calendar to do now - so you don't forget!

Smart leaders know that integrating authentic appreciation takes little effort and increases employee engagement and happiness. You may also notice a decrease in sick time, wasted time and employee conflict. Remember, you are the influence that can make it all happen.

Remember:
GENUINE APPRECIATION WILL PAY FOR ITSELF IN COMPANY LOYALTY OVER AND OVER AGAIN.

Chapter Twelve

CREATE A LEGACY

As we look ahead into the next century, leaders will be those who empower others.   - Bill Gates

Smart leaders create a legacy. They understand that by empowering others we create teams that succeed instead of employees that sabotage.

A boss creates a flock of followers. A boss takes full responsibility for the behaviors and obligations of the employees. The employees fear making mistakes, so they do nothing. Bosses may also take credit for the work of others, but they will never be able to thrive because their time, efforts and energy are limited.

A true leader is not threatened or intimidated by employees who are smart, savvy and innovative. In fact, true leaders go out of their way to attract top talent. They understand that having talented people equals success. They realize that individually we can be good but collectively we can be better.

Your legacy, like mine, is evolving. I finally realized my purpose around age 40 and it's still evolving. The more I learn, grow and achieve, the more I want to learn, grow and achieve. My purpose changes as I continue to grow and yours will also change as you grow.

Bossing people will never empower them to succeed without you. Eventually there will come a time when you won't be in your current position. When you're gone, will you have left a strong, cohesive team who will thrive in your absence? If so, you've left a strong legacy.

What do you want your legacy to be? Take some time now to list what you want to create in your current position and what you want to be remembered for.

_____

_____

_____

_____

_____

_____

_____

_____

_____

Identify the leaders on your team right now (regardless of their titles). What strengths do they bring to your organization? How can you empower them to better use these traits for the benefit of the team?

Leaders	Strength/Talent
_____	_____
_____	_____
_____	_____
_____	_____
_____	_____
_____	_____

Remember:
RECOGNIZE THAT WHEN YOU EMPOWER OTHERS, YOU ALSO EMPOWER YOUR OWN SUCCESS.

Are there areas in your organization that need strong leadership? Which employees could be filling those voids?

Current Voids	Potential Leaders
_____	_____
_____	_____
_____	_____
_____	_____
_____	_____
_____	_____

Smart leaders empower, mentor and create future leaders. Recognize that when you empower others, you also empower your own success. Keep bringing people up to your level, and as long as you continue to improve and evolve, you will boost one another up the leadership ladder.

Bonus Report:
HOW TO HIRE A TEAM FOR SUCCESS

A common complaint of corporations, organizations and small business owners is dealing with staff difficulties and personnel challenges. Your staff holds the key to your business success or failure - they have more interaction with your clients than you do.

Remember, it's so much easier to hire the right people than it is to fire the wrong people. Hiring top talent takes a little more work, but it's well worth the extra time and effort. Here are some tips on how to surround yourself with a team driven toward success:

When you post an open position, share the opening with other professionals whom you respect. Most professionals will not refer someone to you if they would not hire them.

Don't begin your hiring process with individual interviews. Bring in applicants as a group. Ask them to introduce themselves and share one of their unique traits or talents. You'll be able to observe communication skills, how they interact and how they handle an unexpected situation.

This will save hours of interview time and help immediately identify the candidates you want to spend time with in a one-on-one interview.

Never hire someone just because they need a job and you happen to have an opening. To avoid being stuck with an open position, continually be on the lookout for great talent. Interview candidates even when you don't have job openings. Have a comprehensive interview process. Learn as much about the candidate as you possibly can, including how they interact and function at different times of the day and in different workplace environments. Consider personality profiles, background checks and detailed reference checks. Many business owners want to avoid the expense, but trust me, these important tools are well worth the investment and cost far less than hiring someone who damages your business.

If you've made a mistake in hiring, deal with it immediately. Bad employees don't usually improve with time. It's common to avoid problem employees and hope for the best. Do not allow employee saboteurs to damage your business or continue to drain your energy and bank account. Have a probationary or trial period for new hires, and implement a probationary policy if necessary for your current staff.

If the idea of interviewing, hiring and firing overwhelms you, seek out a reputable employment agency. Ask for references and remember to interview agencies as carefully as you would a new employee because they will be an important part of your overall success strategy.

Share goals with your entire staff. Once you've hired great talent, there is a simple way to keep them motivated. Communicate with them as if they are equal partners in the success plan, because they are. Would you like to break a sales record this year? Don't just share this information with top executives, tell the entire staff. There is nothing more motivating than being included a common goal.

Take time away. Leaving your staff in charge shows you trust them and you believe that they can succeed without you.

Beth Caldwell is the creator and lead instructor of Leadership Academy for Women. She is a popular author, speaker and business consultant. Her other books include *I Wish I'd Known THAT! Secrets to Success in Business, EMPOWER* and *Get Paid What You're Worth.* Learn more at **www.Beth-Caldwell.com**.

FAVORITE QUOTES

You manage things; you lead people.
                                 - Rear Admiral Grace Murray Hopper

There is a difference between being a leader and being a boss. Both are based on authority. A boss demands blind obedience; a leader earns his authority through understanding and trust.   - Klaus Balkenhol

Before you are a leader, success is all about growing yourself. When you become a leader, success is all about growing others.   - Jack Welch

Outstanding leaders go out of their way to boost the self-esteem of their personnel. If people believe in themselves, it's amazing what they can accomplish.
                                 - Sam Walton

Wise men talk because they have something to say; fools, because they have to say something.   - Plato

A leader is best when people barely know he exists, when his work is done, his aim fulfilled, they will say: we did it ourselves.   - Lao Tzu

Where there is no vision, the people perish.
- Proverbs 29:18

Life is like a parachute jump, you've got to get it right the first time.
- Eleanor Roosevelt

Sometimes you make the right decision, sometimes you make the decision right.
- Dr. Phil

It's better to be boldly decisive and risk being wrong than to agonize at length and be right too late.
- Marylin Moats Kennedy

Never tell people how to do things. Tell them what to do and they will surprise you with their ingenuity.
- General George Patton

It is the moment of decision that your destiny is shaped.
- Anthony Robbins

In the last analysis, what we are communicates far more eloquently than anything we say or do. *- Stephen Covey*

Any problem, big or small, always seems to start with bad communication. Someone isn't listening.
- Emma Thompson

Managers help people see themselves as they are; Leaders help people to see themselves better than they are.
- Jim Rohn

A real leader faces the music, even when he doesn't like the tune.
- Unknown

You don't need a title to be a leader.
- Unknown

When the effective leader is finished with his work, the people say it happened naturally. — Lao Tzu

Confront issues and challenges – not each other. — Suzanne Mayo Frindt

Leadership is lifting a person's vision to high sights, the raising of a person's performance to a higher standard, the building of a personality beyond its normal limitations. — Peter Drucker

I hate the word failure, but I love the word mistake. — Lisa Gersh

Do what you feel in your heart to be right – for you'll be criticized anyway. — Eleanor Roosevelt

A good leader is a person who takes a little more than his share of the blame and a little less than his share of the credit. — John C. Maxwell

I start with the premise that the function of leadership is to produce more leaders, not more followers. — Ralph Nader

The best executive is the one who has sense enough to pick good men to do what he wants done, and self-restraint enough to keep from meddling with them while they do it. — Theodore Roosevelt

The hallmark of a well-managed organization is not the absence of problems, but whether or not problems are effectively resolved. — Steve Ventura

If your actions create a legacy that inspires others to dream more, learn more, do more and become more, then, you are an excellent leader. — Dolly Parton

A leader is one who sees more than others see, who sees farther than others see, and who sees before others see.
- Leroy Eimes

The only safe ship in a storm is leadership.
- Faye Wattleton

Leadership is influence.
- John C. Maxwell

The greatest leader is not necessarily the one who does the greatest things. He is the one that gets the people to do the greatest things.
- Ronald Reagan

A leader isn't someone who forces others to make him stronger; a leader is someone willing to give his strength to others that they may have the strength to stand on their own.
- Beth Revis

Don't follow the crowd, let the crowd follow you.
- Margaret Thatcher

No man will make a great leader who wants to do it all himself, or to get all the credit for doing it.
- Andrew Carnegie

Victory has a thousand fathers, but defeat is an orphan.
- John F. Kennedy

Example is not the main thing in influencing others. It is the only thing.
- Albert Schweitzer

People do what people see.
- John C. Maxwell

A leader takes people where they want to go. A great leader takes people where they don't necessarily want to go, but ought to be.
- Rosalynn Carter

The real leader has no need to lead - he is content to point the way. — Henry Miller

One of the true tests of leadership is the ability to recognize a problem before it becomes an emergency. — Arnold H. Glasgow

The leader has to be practical and a realist yet must talk the language of the visionary and the idealist. — Eric Hoffer

Leaders think and talk about the solutions. Followers think and talk about the problems. — Brian Tracy

Education is the mother of leadership. — Wendell Willkie

Great leaders are almost always great simplifiers, who can cut through argument, debate, and doubt to offer a solution everybody can understand. — General Colin Powell

People quit people, they don't quit companies. — John C. Maxwell

A man who wants to lead the orchestra must turn his back on the crowd. — Max Lucado

RESOURCES

Develop a Strong Team

The book **Conscious Capitalism: Liberating the Heroic Spirit of Business** by John Mackey is a fascinating look at how some of today's best-known companies including The Container Store, Whole Foods Market, Southwest Airlines, Google, Patagonia, UPS and Costco are transforming both business and society for the good of all.

Vision Alignment is a world-wide licensee of Professional DynaMetric Programs, Inc. (PDP) Their programs train companies on how to align an individual's natural behavior to drive optimal individual and team performance. www.vision-alignment.com.

East Vision Partners helps companies create and maintain ecologically conscious personal and professional development. Their solutions are organizations seeking maximum performance and productivity along with professional and personal fulfillment – and doing so with care for the Earth's living systems. This ecocentric perspective guides our coaching and facilitation processes of inspiring visions and building bridges. Learn more at www.EastVisionPartners.com.

Never Stop Learning

This book, **The 21 Irrefutable Laws of Leadership: Follow Them and People Will Follow You** by John C. Maxwell, is one of the best selling leadership books of all time. It's available in all bookstores.

This website **www.PickTheBrain.com** offers a weekly email newsletter called Grow Yourself. It includes positive thoughts and expert advice.

Dr. Ann Gatty is a business learning specialist. She offers a number of helpful articles and resources here: www.drsgattypeoplesolutions.com/articles.html.

Stop Doing

Simple Mind is an easy-to-use mind mapping tool that turns your computer into a brainstorming, idea collection and thought structuring device to enhance your productivity.

The website **MindTools** offers free online tools for delegation, problem solving and project management. Download a free delegation worksheet here: www.mindtools.com/rs/Delegation.

If You Want It Done Right, You Don't Have to Do It Yourself!: The Power of Effective Delegation is a easy to read and very entertaining book. Author Donna M. Genett, Ph.D., uses a narrative about identical cousins, James and Jones, to introduce her successful six-step program for effective delegation. Whether you are the one delegating or you wish to help your boss become a better delegator, these six simple steps are guaranteed to lighten your workload and give you more time to focus on what's really important on and off the job. Available in bookstores and on Kindle.

Create a Positive Work Environment

Green Design Innovation is owned by the talented and very creative Catherine Montague who works with clients globally. Her company is accredited with the US Green Building Council. Catherine and her team understand that A positive work environment is inherent to running a successful business. Learn more at www.greendesigninnovation.com.

Evy Severino, ACC, SPHR is an executive coach and consultant that helps companies address hinderances. One of her specialities is helping organizations create their own success culture. Learn more here: www.severinoconsulting.net.

Communicate With Purpose

Toastmasters International is a world leader in communication and leadership development with close to 300,000 members worldwide. A Toastmasters meeting is a learn-by-doing workshop in which participants hone their speaking and leadership skills in a no-pressure atmosphere. Club dues average $36 every six months, making this one of the most cost effective skill-building tools available anywhere. www.ToastMasters.org.

Make Up Your Mind

Decisions is an app that will work on your computer or smart phone. The program allows you to keep a list of pros and cons regarding decisions you have to make.

HelpMyDecision.com is a free decision online tool to help with tough decisions. www.helpMYdecision.com.

The book **Outthink the Competition** proves that business competition is undergoing a fundamental paradigm shift and that during such revolutions, outthinkers beat traditionalists. Written by Kaihan Krippendorff and available at bookstores or at www.kaihan.net.

Manage Your Life Instead of Your Time

Patty Kreamer is a Certified Professional Organizer® who has a number of books and resources on her website. My favorites are **But I Might Need it Someday** and **The Power of Simplicity**. Available online at www.ByeByeClutter.com.

SelfControl is a free MAC application to help you avoid distracting websites. www.SelfControlApp.com.

Freedom is a similar application that works on both Windows and MAC computers. If online distractions kill your productivity, Freedom could be the best 10 dollars you'll ever spend. www.macfreedom.com.

The legendary **Eat That Frog! 21 Great Ways to Stop Procrastinating and Get More Done in Less Time** book by Brian Tracy provides the most effective methods for conquering procrastination and accomplishing more. I prefer the audio version to listen to while I'm driving. This is an invaluable resource that should be a part of your company success library.

The Container Store offers more than more than 10,000 innovative products to help customers save space and, ultimately, save them time. They have stores in the US and Canada or you can shop online at www.containerstore.com.

W⁵ Templates offers project management and organizational templates that are easy to use, customized and cost effective. Get a free trial on their website here: www.crmexceltemplate.com.

Don't Hide from Conflict

Living a Championship Life book by Dr. Rick Goodman is available in Paper Book, eBook, MP3 Download, or 2-CD Set. Also check out his helpful webinars on the topic of conflict on his website: www.rickgoodman.com/store.

Become Comfortable with Criticism

Toxic Criticism: Break the Cycle with Friends, Family, Coworkers and Yourself, an e-book by Dr. Eric Maisel. Available on Kindle.

Learn to Negotiate

Women Don't Ask: Negotiation and the Gender Divide, a book written by Linda Babcock and Sara Laschever. Available at all bookstores.

Negotiation Academy for Women at Carnegie Mellon University is the first program in the country to look at critical leadership skills through a negotiation lens. Tailored for the working woman who wants to expand her influence. www.heinz.cmu.edu.

Simple Appreciation

Hinda Incentives offers expert merchandising solutions. They are cutting edge, and will assemble the finest assortment of merchandise awards from the top brand-name manufacturers. They monitor trends and are the first company that I know about which offers digital gifts. They also offer programs to recognize employee wellness. www.hinda.com.

21st Century Employee Assistance Program (EAP) Often the services provided by an EAP to employees and their dependents can address problems and stressors that otherwise diminish job performance. www.21stcenturyeap.com.

Create Your Leadership Legacy

Thoughtback is an application for your computer or smart phone that collects organizes and emails your thoughts, questions and inspiring quotes back to you. It's auto-magic. Available in your app store.

Access the free **Creating Legacy Kit** from Dolly Garlo, RN, JD, PCC-BCC, President of Thrive, Inc. which includes The 14 Elements of Great Legacies e-course along with a fantastic audio recording. www.creatinglegacy.com

About Beth Caldwell

When she received her first leadership position at age 22, Beth Caldwell thought that leadership meant that she was to answer all the questions and provide all the answers. She soon realized that in order to develop a successful and dynamic team, she needed to become a successful leader.

Since that first position, Beth has continued to learn and grow. Today she is a popular author, speaker and workshop facilitator. She is the founder and Executive Director of Pittsburgh Professional Women, a resource organization for professionals and the founder and lead teacher for Leadership Academy for Women. She's won numerous community and professional awards and is a contributing writer for the Pittsburgh Business Times.

About Leadership Academy

Pittsburgh Professional Women launched a new innovative leadership coaching and training program for aspiring women leaders in Western Pennsylvania. The twelve week program is designed to help women understand their leadership style, develop authentic leadership skills, and learn to lead others effectively. The first class graduated in July of 2013.

Beginning in 2014, classes will be available virtually so that women can attend from anywhere in the world. Learn more online here: www.pittsburghprofessionalwomen.org/leadership-academy.

Made in the USA
Columbia, SC
05 May 2018